Bilingual Edition
My Library of Holidays™
Edición Bilingüe

Daryl Heller
Traducción al español:
Tomás González

The Rosen Publishing Group's
PowerKids Press™ & **Editorial Buenas Letras**™
New York

1

For Gabs

Published in 2004 by The Rosen Publishing Group, Inc.
29 East 21st Street, New York, NY 10010

Copyright © 2004 by The Rosen Publishing Group, Inc.

First Edition

Book Design: Michael J. Caroleo

Photo Credits: Cover and pp. 19, 22 (Kinara) © Index Stock; p. 5 © Hakim Mutlaq; p. 7 © GeoAtlas; p. 9 Seattle Art Museum/CORBIS; pp. 11, 22 (fruit) © Michelle Garrett/CORBIS; pp. 13, 21, 22 (candles) © SuperStock; pp. 15, 22 (Unity Cup) © Royalty-Free/CORBIS; pp. 17, 22 (corn) © Tom Stewart/CORBIS; p. 22 (dashiki) courtesy of Daryl Heller.

Heller, Daryl
Kwanzaa / Daryl Heller ; translated by Tomás González.
p. cm. — (My library of holidays)
Includes bibliographical references and index.
Summary: This book introduces the observance of Kwanzaa, a celebration of the cultural heritage of African Americans.
ISBN 1-4042-7528-2 (lib.)
1. Kwanzaa—Juvenile literature 2. African Americans—Social life and customs—Juvenile literature
[1. Kwanzaa   2. Holidays   3. African Americans—Social life and customs
4. Spanish language materials—Bilingual]
I. Title   II. Series
GT4403.A2 H4513 2004   2003-010274
394.261—dc21

Manufactured in the United States of America

Contents

Contenido

Maulana Karenga came up with the idea for a holiday called Kwanzaa in 1966.

En 1966, Maulana Karenga propuso la idea de celebrar una fiesta que se llamaría Kwanzaa.

He wanted African Americans to learn about their African past.

Maulana quería que los afroamericanos aprendieran sobre su pasado africano.

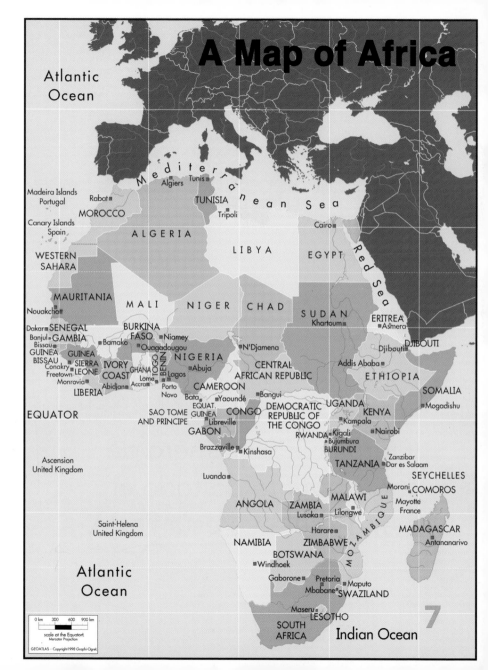

A Map of Africa

Atlantic
Ocean

Mediterranean Sea

Algiers   Tunis

Madeira Islands
Portugal   Rabat

MOROCCO

Canary Islands
Spain

TUNISIA

Tripoli

Cairo

WESTERN
SAHARA

ALGERIA

LIBYA

EGYPT

Red Sea

MAURITANIA

Nouakchott

MALI   NIGER   CHAD

SUDAN

Khartoum

ERITREA

Asmera

Dakar SENEGAL   BURKINA
Banjul GAMBIA   FASO   Niamey
Bissau   Bamako   Ouagadougou
GUINEA
BISSAU   GUINEA   N'Djamena
Conakry SIERRA   IVORY GHANA   NIGERIA
Freetown LEONE   COAST   Lagos   Abuja
Monrovia   Lome Accra   Porto
Abidjan   Novo
LIBERIA   Bata   Yaoundé
CAMEROON
EQUAT.
EQUATOR   SAO TOME GUINEA CONGO
AND PRINCIPE   Libreville
GABON

DJIBOUTI

Djibouti

Addis Ababa

CENTRAL
AFRICAN REPUBLIC

ETHIOPIA

SOMALIA

Mogadishu

Bangui

DEMOCRATIC UGANDA
REPUBLIC OF   KENYA
THE CONGO   Kampala
RWANDA Kigali   Nairobi
Bujumbura
BURUNDI

Brazzaville Kinshasa

Ascension
United Kingdom

Luanda

Zanzibar
TANZANIA Dar es Salaam

SEYCHELLES

Moroni COMOROS

Saint-Helena
United Kingdom

ANGOLA   ZAMBIA

Lusaka

MALAWI

Lilongwe

Mayotte
France

MADAGASCAR

Harare

Antananarivo

NAMIBIA   ZIMBABWE

BOTSWANA

Windhoek

MOZAMBIQUE

Atlantic
Ocean

Gaborone   Pretoria
Mbabane   Maputo
SWAZILAND

Maseru   LESOTHO
SOUTH
AFRICA   Indian Ocean

7

0 km   300   600   900 km

scale at the Equator†
Mercator Projection

GEOATLAS · Copyright1998 Graphi-Ogre†

The seven days of Kwanzaa begin on December 26 and end on January 1. People all around the world honor this holiday.

Los siete días de Kwanzaa empiezan el 26 de diciembre y terminan el primero de enero. Gente de todo el mundo celebra esta fiesta.

December 2003

S	M	T	W	T	F	S
	1	2	3	4	5	6
7	8	9	10	11	12	13
14	15	16	17	18	19	20
21	22	23	24	25	26	27
28	29	30	31			

January 2004

S	M	T	W	T	F	S
				1	2	3
4	5	6	7	8	9	10
11	12	13	14	15	16	17
18	19	20	21	22	23	24
25	26	27	28	29	30	31

9

Kwanzaa comes from a Swahili word that means "first fruits." Farmers of long ago were happy when their fully grown trees gave them fruit.

Kwanzaa es una palabra de la lengua suajili que significa "primeros frutos". Los antiguos granjeros se sentían felices cuando sus árboles crecían y les daban frutos.

11

During Kwanzaa family members think about the seven Kwanzaa ideas. One idea is that people should take care of each other.

Durante la fiesta de Kwanzaa los miembros de la familia piensan sobre las siete ideas de esta fiesta. Una de las ideas dice que las personas deben cuidarse unas a otras.

13

There are seven symbols of Kwanzaa. A symbol is something that stands for an idea. The Unity Cup stands for the idea that people are stronger when they stay together.

La fiesta de Kwanzaa tiene siete símbolos. Un símbolo es algo que representa una idea. La Copa de la Unidad representa la idea de que la gente es más fuerte cuando permanece unida.

Ears of corn are placed on the table at Kwanzaa. There is one ear of corn for each child in the family.

Durante la fiesta de Kwanzaa se ponen mazorcas de maíz en la mesa. Se coloca una mazorca por cada niño que hay en la familia.

17

The kinara holds seven candles. One candle is lit during each night of the holiday.

Un candelabro llamado kinara sostiene siete velas. En cada una de las siete noches que dura la fiesta se enciende una vela.

19

Many African Americans wear African clothing on Kwanzaa. This little boy and his brother each wear a long shirt that is called a dashiki.

En la fiesta de Kwanzaa muchos negros norteamericanos se ponen vestidos africanos. Este niño y su hermano visten las camisas largas llamadas dashikis.

Words to Know
Palabras que debes saber

candles
velas

corn
maíz

dashiki

fruit
frutos

kinara

Unity Cup
Copa de la Unidad

Here are more books to read about Kwanzaa /
Otros libros que puedes leer sobre Kwanzaa:

In English/En inglés:
A Kwanzaa Holiday Cookbook
(Festive Foods for the Holidays)
By Emily Raabe

A Kwanzaa Celebration
By Nancy Williams, Robert Sabuda, illustrator

Due to the changing nature of Internet links, PowerKids Readers has developed an online list of Web sites related to the subject of Kwanzaa. This site is updated regularly. Please use this link to access the list.

http://www.buenasletraslinks.com/mlholi/kwa

Index

C
candle(s), 18
corn, 16

D
dashiki, 20

I
ideas, 12

K
Karenga,
  Maulana, 4
kinara, 18

S
symbols, 14

U
Unity Cup, 14

Índice

C
Copa de la
  Unidad, 14

D
dashiki, 20

I
ideas, 12

K
Karenga,
  Maulana, 4
kinara, 18

M
maíz, 16

S
símbolos, 14

V
vela(s), 18

Words in English: 182   Palabras en español: 209

Note to Parents, Teachers, and Librarians

PowerKids Readers books *en español* are specially designed for emergent Hispanic readers and students learning Spanish in the United States. Simple stories and concepts are paired with photographs of real kids in real-life situations. Sentences are short and simple, employing a basic vocabulary of sight words, as well as new words that describe familiar things and places. With their engaging stories and vivid photo-illustrations, PowerKids *en español* gives children the opportunity to develop a love of reading and learning that they will carry with them throughout their lives.